Will the Pain Ever Go Away?

ALICE LAWSON COX

NAVPRESS

A DIVISION OF THE NAVIGATORS

P.O. BOX 6000, COLORADO SPRINGS, COLORADO 80934

NavPress publishes materials with practical and spiritual insights for everyday living.

ISBN 08910-96485

QUESTIONS WOMEN ASK series edited by Judith Couchman.

This series helps women explore practical and spiritual answers to urgent questions.

Printed in the United States of America

CONTENTS

To Jane and Ellen,
sisters who have shared my pain and joy,
and to Jean,
who cried when I couldn't.

Learn weeping, and thou
shalt gain laughing.
—GEORGE HERBERT, *Jacula Prudentum*

ACKNOWLEDGMENTS

Special thanks to Judith Couchman, editor and encourager, for her words of wisdom.

And thanks to the Morning Glories for their faithful prayers. ∎

Stranded in the Desert of Pain

How this study will help you survive.

I 've been thinking a lot about our getting married," said the young man sitting next to me. "And I've decided I can't marry you, so I can never see you again."

For all my intuition, I never felt it coming. Like a karate chop to the neck, the words blackened my vision and stunned my senses.

As I fingered his grandfather's gold wedding band on a chain around my neck, I recalled his promise six months earlier: "Wear this until I can get you something better."

Now my dreams—our dreams—of wedding festivities, romantic nights, and laughing children vanished like a mirage.

"What about all the times you said you loved me?" I asked between sobs.

The words hit solidly: "I guess I was just infatuated."

Greeted by Tears

Almost every woman knows the anguish of loss. At some point in most lives, death, divorce, or destroyed relationships invade our world and leave us aching and alone. As we look out on a desert of pain, only scorched sand and salty tears greet us.

If you've known emotional or physical pain that won't leave, this booklet is for you. It will help you find your way out of the desert. Like a map, it unfolds "the big picture" and offers avenues of escape. However, you're not ready for an escape route if you're too weak to move. So you'll need a water bottle—and I've supplied that for you, too.

Here's how this booklet works. First, an article maps out and explores the question, "Will the pain ever go away?" Then four short lessons help sort your feelings and introduce the spiritual aspect of relieving pain. They function as the water bottle because these lessons are based on refreshing stories from God's word, the Bible.

You needn't worry if you're unfamiliar with the Bible, or if you feel uneasy about studying what it says. Excerpts from the Bible appear in the lessons, so you need only a pencil and this booklet. And the lessons can be studied in whatever way you wish: by yourself, with a friend, or in a group.

Whatever you read, however you study, let this booklet bring comfort and help you deal with the hurt in your life.

Will the pain go away? For some, yes. For others, not entirely. Either way, let's walk through this desert together. I see the shade of a tree just ahead. ■

— ALICE LAWSON COX

Will I Ever Be Happy Again?

Why suffering can overwhelm you.

M y alarm clock blared, and I cocked a weary eye at it — 7 a.m. *I can't do it,* I thought. *I just can't face another day.*

I groped for the snooze button, mashed it, then closed my eyes. As I rolled over in bed, my thoughts drifted to childhood vacations and body surfing at the beach. But instead of happy times splashing in the water, the waves felt menacing and my family far away.

In my mind I was near the shore, constantly jumping over the waves so they wouldn't smash into my face. Up and over, up and over. Occasionally I dived into a wave to avoid the brunt of its already curling, white foam. The surf roared in my ears.

But the waves were getting higher, and I couldn't keep up the game much longer. I feared that soon I'd be sucked under and my face would slam into the grainy sand. Then, breathless, my lungs would fill with salty water.

The alarm sounded again. Just like in my half-awake dream, I felt the morning and its responsibilities dragging me under. Down,

down, down. I was drowning in an ocean of pain, with nobody to pull me out.

As I punched my pillow I wondered, *Will I ever feel happy again? Will this pain ever go away?*

Multiple Agonies

Two weeks earlier I had squeezed my mother's cold hand, then watched two white-uniformed men wheel away her lifeless body. She had fought lung cancer bravely, just as my father had faced leukemia years before. But in the end, both had lost. They had left me an orphan — with no parents, no home, no direction.

Then, as if this pain wasn't enough, a good friend crashed his car into a telephone pole a week after my mother's death. Earl died, leaving behind a young widow and a seven-year-old daughter. The seeming senselessness of his death left me reeling.

"It's not fair!" I had sobbed over and over, tears streaming down my cheeks.

Now phantoms of Earl and my parents paraded in my mind as I lay in bed. I blinked and looked out the window. The budding trees and new life of spring outside mocked the hollowness within me. How did the sun dare rise and birds sing as if things had not changed? How could I be expected to eat and sleep and laugh in a world where these loved ones could not join me?

Somehow I had to find a way to outlast the pain. Somehow. One day. But not this day. The waves were getting higher.

Before these deaths, I had thought I understood pain. In college, I'd studied tragedies in literature. Then as part of my job for nearly four years, I'd visited prisoners and written about their lives. I'd listened to women who had been raped, and I'd talked with men on death row. In my private life, I had sheltered women from abusive husbands and lent an ear when a colleague's wife ran off with another man.

I'd certainly witnessed pain, but now I was living it. None of my studying or sympathizing had prepared me for the agony—or the listlessness—I felt now. The accumulated grief weighed me down.

Why did this have to happen? Why was I left behind? Could I ever really smile again? As I fell back asleep, returning to the only peace I knew, these questions haunted me.

Many Faces of Pain

"He has seen but half the universe who never has been shown the house of Pain," said the poet, Ralph Waldo Emerson.[1] As much as we'd like to avoid it, pain is an integral part of the human experience. Just as no one escapes death, so no one hides from pain. It hits in many different ways, pointing to our fragility and mortality. It can devastate us physically, emotionally, mentally, spiritually.

Physical pain. When we were children, a kiss on a scraped knee made physical pain "all better." My grandmother even had a "magic blanket" to wrap me in when I hurt.

But any woman who's suffered through chronic illness, an unfortunate accident, or a life-threatening disease, knows that kisses and

11

magic blankets, no matter how tender, do not wipe away pain.

In an article in *Worldwide Challenge,* Beth Lueders, who has suffered two car accidents and a debilitating fall, described the anguish of physical pain. She wrote: "I'm afraid of more tests, more doctors, more pain, more time off work, more bed rest, more debt, more paperwork, more legal complications, more tears, more lonely times, more insurance hassles, more false hope. . . ."

For Beth, pain and discouragement are a daily reality, making her wonder sometimes if she can "endure another moment of fighting to break free from the grip of the silent tormentor."[2]

Emotional pain. Emotional pain can be as wrenching as its physical counterpart, and sometimes more lasting. Psychologists tell us that people who were abused as children often bear the emotional scars into old age. Perhaps this explains why more than half of the women in American prisons say they have been physically abused and more than one-third have been sexually abused.[3]

Verbal abuse also causes emotional pain. As a child, one of my friend's parents constantly told her, "You're dumb!" Even though she now holds a master's degree and a prestigious job, she feels she never measures up to their standards. Her constant busyness and overachieving reflect a ceaseless grasping for their approval. She harbors ongoing emotional wounds.

Mental pain. Just as we can't separate ourselves from emotional and physical pain,

12

so we can't turn off our minds. Mental pain includes guilt, remorse, confusion, doubts, and frustration. Often we let our failures chafe us. Internally, we lament that we have hurt people we love, realizing how our selfishness and wrong choices offended them. We continue to kick ourselves for things done long ago.

When my friend Jane left an abusive husband, afraid for her life, she suffered from nagging doubts. For years she asked herself, *How could I be such a failure? What will people think of me?*

Spiritual pain. Closely intertwined with our physical nature is the spiritual side, our essence. The spirit is the thinking, motivating, feeling part of a person. It's what left my mother's body when she gasped her last breath. One minute I was looking at my mother, the next, staring at the shell that had housed her soul.

Frequently the death of a loved one, or the realization of our own mortality, spurs us to examine this spiritual aspect. Suffering a loss can make us search for lasting answers.

Often the pain we can't pinpoint is, in reality, a spiritual hunger. It's a longing to be known and loved unconditionally. It's a question about the purpose of life, an intuition that maybe our souls can live on without our bodies. If we allow it, spiritual pain can initiate our search for someone greater than ourselves.

Ways We Cope
Our responses to pain vary as much as the ways we are hurt. Sometimes we seek comfort in wine. Or we numb ourselves with Valium®

13

or a vial of crack. We crave sex or take death-defying risks.

Other methods of coping aren't quite so destructive. For example, a friend whose daughter was murdered screams on a deserted beach late at night. I eat to excess and indulge in therapy shopping. Some people brood and fall silent. Others deny that anything is wrong.

But whatever the hurt, whatever our reaction, pain must be acknowledged and dealt with. Whether pain is physical, emotional, mental, or spiritual, we must grieve to recover from it. We must claim our circumstances instead of letting our circumstances claim us.[4] Our wholeness depends on it.

More Than Time

The first step in working through pain is to admit we're hurting. We must face facts, acknowledge that something or someone is gone and that life will never be quite the same.

In the novel *Longshot*, a mystery by Dick Francis, the main character found himself in a life-threatening situation. Recalling books he had written about survival, the hero said, "The first rule of surviving a disaster . . . is to accept that it had happened and make the best of what was left. Self-pity, regrets, hopelessness and surrender would never get one home."[5]

Americans have a difficult time accepting pain. It runs counter to our ideas about the Land of Opportunity and fantasies like Disney World. And while other cultures have rituals and symbolic dress for grieving, we are taught to bury our feelings and suffer alone.

14

Yet to progress through pain, we must learn to admit how we feel and to confide in others whom we can trust. Anger, frustration, fear, and sadness are all emotions connected with pain. If these feelings are allowed free expression, they will pass much sooner.

So the key to recovery is not composure, but honesty. When we deny feelings, they resurface at odd times in unpleasant ways. A friend of mine who never worked through her sister's death poses an unfortunate example: She's now in a clinic for drug and alcohol abuse.

Sometimes people encourage us to keep a stiff upper lip, to act happy when we feel miserable. They insist we can replace the loss, or tell us "It's not so bad, just give it time." They mean well, but display their naiveté. As the publisher Henry George Bohn said, "He preaches patience who never knew pain."[6]

Time does heal wounds, but only when we use that time to grieve and to confront the pain and its manifestations.

Honest Assessments

On the other hand, release from pain requires an honest assessment of its cause. Because bitterness can destroy us, we must forgive the ones who hurt us. For example, adult children of alcoholics are taught to mentally separate the parent from the disease. This does not mean endorsing wrong deeds, but forgiving the ill person.

By the same token, we must claim responsibility for our own actions that contributed to the pain. Release from pain may also mean forgiving ourselves for the wrongs we have done. Here lies the value of Christianity. Only when we comprehend the depth of God's love for us, despite our sins, can we truly accept his forgiveness.

As we seek the cleansing that Jesus Christ offers, we let go of our guilt. As we learn to trust him, we release our fears and doubts. We find inner peace when we find his lasting answers—answers that take us beyond the pain and give us a reason to live anew.

When we allow ourselves to grieve and take appropriate actions, we allow ourselves to be healed—eventually. Over time we dwell less on pain, more on hope. We find small things for which to be grateful. We gain new perspectives and priorities. Sometimes, we even grow to see the positive aspects of our season of sorrow.

A Terrible Beauty

Regardless of our response, the experience of suffering alters us. In the poem "Easter 1916," which commemorates martyrs in Ireland's fight for freedom, William Butler Yeats said, "All changed, changed utterly, a terrible beauty is born."[7] Like the people of Dublin whom Yeats described, everyone who experiences pain is changed. Time heals, but the healed person is different from the one with no scars.

My friend Jill, who's grieving the death of an infant son, has learned that pain can make people more compassionate.

"You can tell the people who have been through hard times, because they reach out," she said. "A lot of friends avoid me as if it

16

might happen to them. Others talk about replacement babies, thinking children are interchangeable. I've learned a lot about comforting others, about just being there for them."

Jill has also learned the value of silence. Some pain runs so deep that words are insufficient. Hugs and handclasps speak eloquently.

Through the death of their son, Jill and her husband have gained a keener appreciation for life and its finiteness. "Next time," she said, "if there is a next time, I won't take for granted a healthy baby—or complain about him crying at night."

Sometimes we are changed in ways we don't see. People notice in us a stronger character born from our trials. We reach out to others in a strength secretly forged during our grief.

Where It Leads

At first we react to pain instinctively—with anger, isolationism, numbness. But over time, we can determine our responses and how we will let pain change us. We can choose bitterness or compassion, self-pity or hope. We can even allow loneliness and helplessness to steer us where we might not have ventured before.

C. S. Lewis, the Oxford don and author, said, "God whispers to us in our pleasures, speaks in our conscience, but shouts in our pains: it is His megaphone to rouse a deaf world."[8]

If we've been deaf to God, pain can spur us to venture into his vast, unconditional love. At first we may curse God, naming him as the cause of our pain. We may continuously ask "Why?" But, if we choose, we can turn our

questions from "Why?" to "Who?" As we seek
to find out who God is, we discover he is a faithful comforter and a loving father.

Beyond the Pain

God's comfort is available to everyone who asks.
As we rely on his love, we find strength to face
each day's pain. He carries our burdens and
promises some day to wipe away all pain.

As we gain a perspective on eternity, we
realize pain is only for a while. Nature's cycle of
seasons reminds us that even the harshest win-
ter has a purpose. Seeds lie dormant, but alive,
under the frozen earth. Spring always arrives;
our waiting is not in vain.

Right now you're in a season of pain, won-
dering if it will ever go away. Although you
can't hurry or avoid painful circumstances, you
can choose steps to ease the hurt. Reading this
booklet is one; finding out more about God and
his promises is another. Both reach toward life
and wholeness.

The other day I baked bread—a seemingly
small feat. But as I punched dough instead of
my pillow, I knew my season of sorrow was
coming to a close. My energy had returned,
replacing selfishness with a desire to give.

Later, as I smelled the warm earthiness
of baking yeast, I smiled. The heat from the
oven brought a flush to my face, and another
memory from childhood drifted through my
mind. I remembered my family eating together
at the dinner table.

Give us, Lord, our daily bread, I thought. And
I knew I was ready to partake in life again. ■

NOTES

1. Burton Stevenson, ed., *The Home Book of Quotations* (New York: Dodd, Mead and Company, 1967), page 1444.
2. Beth Lueders, "Through the Pain," *Worldwide Challenge,* January/February 1991, pages 20-21.
3. Statistics cited from a survey of 2,094 female inmates conducted by the American Correctional Association in November and December, 1987.
4. Definition of recovery from John W. James and Frank Cherry, *The Grief Recovery Handbook: A Step-by-Step Program for Moving Beyond Loss* (New York: Harper & Row, Publishers, 1988), page 4.
5. Dick Francis, *Longshot* (New York: Putnam, 1990), page 293.
6. H. L. Mencken, ed., *A New Dictionary of Quotations* (New York: Alfred A. Knopf, 1942), page 881.
7. William Butler Yeats, "Easter 1916," *Selected Poems and Two Plays of William Butler Yeats,* M. L. Rosenthal ed. (New York: Collier Books, 1966).
8. C. S. Lewis, *The Problem of Pain* (New York: Macmillan, 1977), page 93.

Prescription for Pain Relief

Learn from an ancient
book of comfort.

You've read about surviving painful times, but
don't stop here. The Bible says a lot more about
pain—and how God can help you through it.
So despite your pain-inflicted inertia, take a few
moments to complete the following four lessons.

Each lesson focuses on one or two women
in the Bible. The studies make four assump-
tions, explained by the Bible verses in italics.

1. God exists. *The living God is among you*
(Joshua 3:10). His Son, Jesus, was God's repre-
sentative to people on earth. *And a voice came
from heaven: "You [Jesus] are my Son, whom I love,
with you I am well pleased"* (Luke 3:22).

2. God cares about you. He wants to be
part of your daily life, especially when you're
afraid. *"Do not fear, for I am with you; do not be
dismayed, for I am your God. I will strengthen you
and help you"* (Isaiah 41:10).

**3. The Bible holds God's words to human-
ity.** *All Scripture is God-breathed and is useful for*

teaching, rebuking, correcting and training (2 Timothy 3:16).

4. God will help change you for the better if you ask him into your life. *For it is God who works in you to will and to act according to his good purpose* (Philippians 2:13).

Even if you're skeptical, even if you don't understand everything, try the lessons. They'll help you understand yourself better. And introduce you to a personal God who loves you and understands your pain. ∎

Why Me, Lord?

Love in the midst of difficulties.

M y Goal: *To understand the source of my pain. Examples: Hannah, a barren woman who longed for a child; and a criminal facing execution.*

Have you ever cried so much you couldn't eat? Hannah did. At the time when she lived, about 1100 BC, a Hebrew woman's worth depended on the number of children she bore. And Hannah had none.

Hannah's husband said he loved her as much as ten sons would, but she wasn't consoled. The Bible tells this story in the Old Testament book of 1 Samuel. It continues:

> In bitterness of soul Hannah wept much and prayed to the LORD. And she made a vow, saying, "O LORD Almighty, if you will only look upon your servant's misery and remember me, and not forget your servant but give her a son, then I will give him to the LORD for all the days of his life. . . ."
>
> Hannah was praying in her heart, and her lips were moving but her voice was not heard.

[The priest] Eli thought she was drunk. . . .
  "Not so, my lord," Hannah replied, "I
am a woman who is deeply troubled. . . .
I was pouring out my soul to the LORD. . . .
I have been praying here out of my great
anguish and grief."
  Eli answered, "Go in peace, and may the
God of Israel grant you what you have asked of
him." (1 Samuel 1:10-11,13,15-17)

Intense Feelings

Hannah's prayers were so fervent that the priest confused them with drunken mumblings.

1. If you were in Hannah's situation, what feelings would cause you pain?

2. What might have been Hannah's motivation for passionately praying directly to God?

Nobody to Blame

Many times, as in Hannah's situation, the pain we feel isn't our fault. Circumstances or other

24

people bring pain upon us. Other times, we bring pain upon ourselves. For example, a man who lived in Jesus Christ's day made a mistake that cost him his life.

We find this man's story in the New Testament book of Luke:

> *When they came to the place called the Skull, there they crucified him [Jesus], along with the criminals — one on his right, the other on his left.*
>
> *Jesus said, "Father, forgive them, for they know not what they are doing." . . .*
>
> *One of the criminals who hung there hurled insults at him: "Aren't you the Christ? Save yourself and us!"*
>
> *But the other criminal rebuked him. "Don't you fear God," he said, "since you are under the same sentence? We are punished justly, for we are getting what our deeds deserve. But this man has done nothing wrong."* (Luke 23:33-34,39-41)

3. a. Jesus and the two criminals were in agony, dying because each was nailed to a cross. Compare the three men according to their responses to suffering.

   Jesus:

First criminal:

Second criminal:

b. By each man's name, write whether he was "guilty" or "not guilty." What was remarkable about Jesus' response?

About Yourself

4. Now think about your pain.

   a. In what ways do you identify with Hannah?

b. In what ways do you identify with either of the two criminals or with Jesus?

5. What would you like to say to God about your pain?

6. a. What do you believe is the cause of your pain?

b. Have any of your actions caused this pain or contributed to it? Explain.

Story Endings

Hannah's story ended happily. God gave her the son she prayed for, and she named him Samuel, meaning "asked of God." True to her promise, Hannah dedicated her son to the Lord and took him to the temple, where he served the priest. Later, God honored the once-barren Hannah by giving her five more children. (See 1 Samuel 2:21.)

Although the criminal died, his story ended with hope. After rebuking his bitter companion, the criminal said to Jesus, "Jesus, remember me when you come into your kingdom."

Jesus forgave the criminal's sin and answered, "I tell you the truth, today you will be with me in paradise" (Luke 23:42-43).

7. a. In the two Bible stories, how did God respond to pain?

   b. In regard to God's response, did it matter that one person brought suffering upon himself and the other didn't? Explain.

8. According to these stories, what attitude elicits a compassionate response from God?

9. If Jesus were to talk to you now, would there be anything in your life that would need forgiveness? Why, or why not?

10. a. From what you've learned in this lesson, write an ending to your painful story.

   b. What might you need to do to reach this end?

Clues to Comfort

Why is there pain, anyway? This week, explore why suffering exists in our world. Completing the lesson, "More Than a Myth," on pages 63-69, will help you understand the origin of pain. ■

Does Anybody Really Care?

There's comfort in times of trial.

M y Goal: *To find comfort and help during pain-ful times. Example: Jesus Christ comforted Mary of Bethany at Lazarus' tomb.*

John Donne, a seventeenth-century poet and priest, wrote, "No man is an island, entire of itself. . . . Any man's death diminishes me, because I am involved in mankind. And, there-fore, never send to know for whom the bell tolls; it tolls for thee."[1] Donne believed we all suffer when the church bells announce some-one's death.

No bells tolled the day Jesus' friend Laz-arus died, but Jesus still felt saddened. By the time he arrived in Bethany (near Jeru-salem) to comfort Lazarus' sisters, Martha and Mary, his friend had been dead for four days.

The Bible narrative continues in the book of John:

When Mary reached the place where Jesus was and saw him, she fell at his feet and said, "Lord, if you had been here, my brother would not have died."

When Jesus saw her weeping, and the Jews who had come along with her also weeping, he was deeply moved in spirit and troubled. "Where have you laid him?" he asked.

"Come and see, Lord," they replied.

Jesus wept.

Then the Jews said, "See how he loved him!" (John 11:32-36)

Searching for Comfort

1. Where did Mary of Bethany find comfort for her brother's death?

2. How do you feel about Jesus' display of emotion during this painful time?

3. List some ways you seek comfort for your
   pain, both healthy and unhealthy.

Healthy	Unhealthy

4. What are some sources of comfort you
   would like to explore?

Comforting Creator

5. The Bible says a lot about comfort. Sometimes God gives us what we ask for; other
   times he strengthens us with his presence
   and love.

   a. The following verses compare God to
      images we're familiar with. After each

verse, describe the nature of the thing or person that provides comfort.

God is our refuge and strength, an ever-present help in trouble. (Psalm 46:1)

"As a mother comforts her child, so will I comfort you." (Isaiah 66:13)

b. How might these descriptions affect your view of God?

6. According to the following verses, what does God do when he comforts us? Write a summary below, after the verses.

The LORD is close to the brokenhearted and saves those who are crushed in spirit. (Psalm 34:18)

"Do not fear for I am with you; do not be dismayed, for I am your God. I will strengthen you and help you; I will uphold you with my righteous right hand." (Isaiah 41:10)

Isaiah prophesied about Jesus: *He [God the Father] has sent me [Jesus] to bind up the brokenhearted . . . to comfort all who mourn, and provide for those who grieve.* (Isaiah 61:1,3)

Looking at You

7. a. How would you like God to comfort you?

b. Write your own image of how God could comfort you.

8. From what you've learned about God so far, how might he respond if you brought your pain to him?

Personal Resurrection

In this lesson's beginning Bible passage, Jesus did more than visit Mary and Martha of Bethany. He went to the tomb of their brother and told the crowd to take away the stone sealing its entrance.

Then, after praying aloud, he called, "Lazarus, come out!" Suddenly the dead man emerged, grave clothes and all.

9. a. Is there something dead in your life that causes you pain? If so, describe it.

b. Have you let anything die because you're in pain? Explain.

10. Do you believe Jesus Christ has the power to resurrect something in your life that is now dead? Why, or why not?

11. What, if anything, could keep you from seeking God's comfort?

Clues to Comfort

The Bible talks a lot about people who despair and people who hope. This week, explore some of these feelings in the book of Psalms, a collection of the songs of God's people. Many were written by David, the second king of Israel.

Read the following passages on the days assigned. Ask God to help you understand what you read.

- Monday: Psalm 23.

- Tuesday: Psalm 25.

- Wednesday: Psalm 32.

- Thursday: Psalm 62.

- Friday: Psalm 116. ■

NOTE
1. Alexander M. Witherspoon, ed., *The College Survey of English Literature* (New York: Harcourt, Brace & World, 1957), pages 340-341.

Can I Be Healed?

Grace extends beyond the pain.

M *y Goal: To move beyond my pain toward heal-ing. Example: A chronically ill woman who believed Jesus Christ could heal her.*

Rumors were flying. Jesus of Galilee had healed many sick people: a woman with a fever, a man with leprosy, a paralytic. As Jesus traveled throughout the region, teaching about God the Father and his kingdom, more and more crowds followed him.

One day a synagogue ruler fell at Jesus' feet and begged him, "My little daughter is dying. Please come and put your hands on her so that she will be healed and live."

Right away Jesus—and his growing entou-rage—set off for the man's home. Along the way, the crowd jostled and pushed to get close to this awesome man Jesus. Everywhere he went, hurting people wanted healing from Jesus.

But just as suddenly as Jesus had started, he stopped. The Bible gives us this account in the book of Mark:

A woman was there who had been subject to bleeding for twelve years. She had suffered a great deal under the care of many doctors and had spent all she had, yet instead of getting better she grew worse.

When she heard about Jesus, she came up behind him in the crowd and touched his cloak, because she thought, "If I just touch his clothes, I will be healed." Immediately her bleeding stopped and she felt in her body that she was freed from her suffering.

At once Jesus realized that power had gone out from him. He turned around in the crowd and asked, "Who touched my clothes?"

"You see the people crowding against you," his disciples answered, "and yet you can ask, 'Who touched me?'"

But Jesus kept looking around to see who had done it. Then the woman, knowing what had happened to her, came and fell at his feet and, trembling with fear, told him the whole truth. He said to her, "Daughter, your faith has healed you. Go in peace and be freed from your suffering." (Mark 5:25-34)

Fear and Faith

According to Jewish law, women were considered unclean during their menstrual periods and were shunned. This woman, who had been bleeding for twelve years, would have been particularly ostracized. Even though she'd spent her last nickel searching for a cure, she'd only gotten worse.

1. How could this woman's pain have caused
   her to express great fear and great faith at
   the same time?

2. In what ways do you identify with this
   woman?

3. a. Jesus said this woman had faith. How
      would you define faith?

b. Why is faith necessary for recovery from painful episodes in our lives?

Expressions of Faith

4. The following Bible verses talk about faith. After each verse, record how this kind of faith (or lack of it) could affect your painful situation.

   He [Jesus] did not do many miracles there because of their lack of faith. (Matthew 13:58)

   We live by faith, not by sight. (2 Corinthians 5:7)

For it is by grace you have been saved, through faith – and this not from yourselves, it is the gift of God – not by works, so that no one can boast. (Ephesians 2:8)

Now faith is being sure of what we hope for and certain of what we do not see. (Hebrews 11:1)

The Gift of Touch

5. People convey many different messages through touching.

   a. What did this woman's touch signify?

   b. Why was her touch different from those of the many other people pressing in on Jesus?

c. How did Jesus respond to the woman's touch?

6. What does touch communicate to you in
your pain?

7. Why do you think Jesus wanted the woman
to acknowledge her actions?

A Responsive Healer

As with most people, the woman's physical
pain had led to emotional pain. Sometimes God
heals us physically and emotionally; sometimes
he heals only our emotions—no small thing!
He promises if we reach out to him, he will
respond.

44

8. In the first part of this booklet, we explored several types of pain (pages 11-13). As you examine your life, where do you sense pain now?

Physical	Emotional

Mental	Spiritual

9. Look back at Mark 5:25-34 at the beginning of this lesson (page 40). In the second to last sentence, the word *healed* actually means "saved" in the original Greek text. What do you think Jesus meant by this?

10. If Jesus Christ were physically in the room with you, how would you express your longing for wholeness?

11. a. What, if anything, is keeping you from accepting wholeness from Jesus?

b. What steps can you take to eliminate this
   barrier?

Clues to Comfort

Write the following verse on several 3" x 5"
cards and place them in prominent places,
such as the refrigerator and bathroom mirror.
As you go about your week, contemplate this
verse and how it can help you move toward
wholeness. See if you can memorize the verse
by week's end.

> *He [Jesus] welcomed them and spoke to them
> about the kingdom of God, and healed those who
> needed healing.* (Luke 9:11) ∎

Why Should I Hope?
Living in the light of healing.

M y Goal: *To live each day with hope. Example: Mary Magdalene, a woman who loved Jesus.*

It was a Sunday in Palestine. For Mary Magdalene and others who followed Jesus, the world seemed to have crashed. Two days earlier, she watched the man who had healed her — the one who had driven seven demons from her (Luke 8:2) — die an excruciating death on a cross.

The Jewish laws concerning the Sabbath (our Saturday) prevented Mary Magdalene from preparing Jesus' body for burial, but this morning, she rose early. The Bible continues the account in the book of John:

Early on the first day of the week, while it was still dark, Mary Magdalene went to the tomb and saw that the stone had been removed from the entrance.

So she came running to Simon Peter and the other disciple [John], the one Jesus loved, and said, "They have taken the Lord out of

*the tomb, and we don't know where they have
put him!" . . . (They still did not understand
from Scripture that Jesus had to rise from
the dead.)*

*. . . Mary stood outside the tomb crying.
As she wept, she bent over to look into the
tomb and saw two angels in white, seated where
Jesus' body had been, one at the head and the
other at the foot.*

*They asked her, "Woman, why are you
crying?"*

*"They have taken my Lord away," she
said, "and I don't know where they have put
him." At this, she turned around and saw Jesus
standing there, but she did not realize that it
was Jesus.*

*"Woman," he said, "why are you crying?
Who is it you are looking for?"*

*Thinking he was the gardener, she said,
"Sir, if you have carried him away, tell me
where you have put him, and I will get him."*

Jesus said to her, "Mary."

*She turned toward him and cried out in
Aramaic, "Rabboni!" (which means Teacher).*
(John 20:1-2,9-16)

The Living Christ

In this account, Mary Magdalene entered the
garden—on what we call Easter—expecting
a dead body. Instead, she found the living
Christ.

1. a. Mary Magdalene did not seem startled
by angels or the "gardener." What

does this say about Mary's resolve to
find Jesus?

b. Have you ever had a similar desire to
ease your pain? Explain.

2. a. List several adjectives that describe
how Mary must have felt when Jesus
addressed her by name.

b. What would this personal expression by
Jesus indicate?

3. Aside from regaining a beloved friendship, what else would Jesus' presence restore for Mary?

4. Jesus was near Mary in her sorrow, but she didn't recognize him. How might you learn to see Jesus in your pain?

Hope and Help

5. According to the following Bible verses, what does Jesus promise to do for humanity when he returns to earth?

He will swallow up death forever. The Sovereign LORD will wipe away the tears from all faces; he will remove the disgrace of his people. (Isaiah 25:8)

"He will wipe every tear from their eyes. There will be no more death or mourning or crying or pain, for the old order of things has passed away." (Revelation 21:4)

6. a. In the meantime, what does God promise for those who follow him?

"I know the plans I have for you," declares the LORD, "plans to prosper you and not to harm you, plans to give you hope and a future. Then you will call upon me and come and pray to me, and I will listen to you. You will seek me and find me when you seek me with all your heart." (Jeremiah 29:11-13)

No eye has seen, no ear has heard, no mind has conceived what God has prepared for those who love him. (1 Corinthians 2:9)

b. How can these promises help you during
   painful times?

Gaining Perspective

7. Stop to ponder what you've studied in these
   lessons. Then quiz yourself on what you
   believe.

Yes No

❏ ❏ I have pain I can't handle by myself.

❏ ❏ I want to do something about my pain.

❏ ❏ When I'm honest, I know that some of
       my pain comes from my wrong actions or
       inability to forgive someone.

❏ ❏ I would like to lean on God and accept his
       peace.

❏ ❏ I am interested in a relationship with God
       and want to learn more about him.

8. People in pain often gain new perspectives
   on what is really important. Take a few min-
   utes to contemplate how pain has changed

your perspective. Think with a pencil in your hand. Write ideas or questions as they come to you.

9. a. How would inviting Jesus into your life give you new hope?

   b. If you're not interested in God's healing yet, what is the reason?

10. If you would like to invite Jesus into your life, read "More Than a Myth" on

pages 63-69, and "The Choice Is Yours" on pages 71-72.

Then below, write a prayer of confession for your sin and acceptance of God's forgiveness. Also ask God to begin healing your pain as you grow to know him better.

Clues to Comfort

This week, meditate on the following poem about Mary Magdalene's encounter with the resurrected Christ. Think about what hope it holds for you, then write your own short verse that gives you hope during pain.

"Mary"

The Love I love
Came in the early dawning
Standing as still as light.

How could I ever have dreamed
So sweet a morning
After so dark a night?[1]

—Elizabeth Rooney ■

NOTE

1. Elizabeth Rooney, "Mary," in *A Widening Light: Poems of the Incarnation* (Wheaton, IL: Harold Shaw, 1984), page 116. Used by permission.

When Chocolate Isn't Enough

Ways to cope with trouble.

N o one ever told me about the laziness of grief," wrote C. S. Lewis in *A Grief Observed*, a diary he kept the first year after his wife's death. "Except at my job—where the machine seems to run on much as usual—I loathe the slightest effort. Not only writing but even reading a letter is too much. Even shaving."[1]

Pain and sorrow sap energy. Don't expect to keep the pace you set before they invaded your world. Be gentle with yourself. Here are some tips to help you through tough times:

- **Get enough sleep.** During hard times your body craves rest. If you want to go to bed at 7:30 p.m., do it. Don't worry about undone tasks: take care of yourself first.

- **Pamper yourself.** If a hot bath sounds good, relax in a sea of bubbles. Treat yourself to a massage. Do something to make yourself smile.

- **Eat right.** It's tempting to ignore good nutrition. Whether you have an appetite or not, eat three healthy meals a day.

- **Exercise regularly.** If you do have energy, use it positively: swim laps, work out, walk. It will get your mind off yourself and your problems. Exercise can also help pull you out of depression.

- **Listen to music.** Classical or instrumental music can be especially soothing.

- **Lower your expectations.** Do only those tasks that *must* be done.

- **Avoid making major decisions.** It's best not to move or change careers for a year. Wait until you're clearheaded.

- **Take one day at a time, one task at a time.** Looking beyond the immediate can be overwhelming. Remember, right now the goal is survival.

- **Give yourself time.** If you are grieving a major loss, you'll need from one to two years of adjustment. ■

NOTE
1. C. S. Lewis, *A Grief Observed* (New York: Bantam Books, 1961), pages 3-4.

The Positive Side of Pain

It warns and protects us.

In the book *Fearfully and Wonderfully Made*, surgeon Paul Brand described the value of pain as a warning system to the body. Regarding leprosy patients, he said:

> The gradual loss of the sense of pain leads to misuse of those body parts most dependent on pain's protection. A person uses a hammer with a splintery handle, does not feel the pain, and an infection flares up. Another steps off a curb spraining an ankle, and keeps walking.[1]

Pain can protect us from harmful things, such as sticking a hand in a flame or staying in an abusive relationship. Pain can point out places that need to be healed. If we hurt enough, we will seek out a doctor, counselor, or minister. Usually, we experience pain before healing. ■

NOTE

1. Paul Brand, M.D., and Philip Yancey, *Fearfully and Wonderfully Made: A Surgeon Looks at the Human and Spiritual Body* (Grand Rapids, MI: Zondervan Publishing House, 1980), page 37.

Good Grief, Bad Grief

How to tell the difference.

Normal Grief

- Insomnia or too much sleep.

- Loss of appetite.

- Weight change: loss or gain.

- Increased or decreased interest in sex.

- Physical complaints: fatigue, dizziness, excessive sweating, skin rashes, heart pains, chest or throat tightness.

- Breathlessness or sighing.

- Lack of energy.

- Unpredictable or erratic behavior; fear of going crazy.

- Crying spells that feel uncontrollable.

- Mood swings.

- Restlessness.

- Inability to concentrate.

- Unforgetfulness.

- Irritability.

Abnormal Grief

- Denial, after a prolonged period, that the loss has occurred.

- Prolonged preoccupation with what was not done or said before the loss.

- No emotions: repression and denial of anger.

- Angry explosions at insignificant events.

- "Frenzied" behaviors; staying excessively busy.

- Physical complaints; new or exacerbated old pains.

- Extreme preoccupation with the loss at second anniversary.

- "Giving-up" attitude of helplessness, hopelessness, or social withdrawal.

- Excessive drinking.

- Suicidal thoughts.

- Excessive, extreme anger toward individuals.[1]

NOTE
1. Paul Meier, M.D., "Moving Through the Stages of Grief," *Christian Psychology for Today*, vol. 6, no. 2, Spring 1990, page 12. Used by permission.

More Than a Myth
The original pain of sin.

P ain hasn't always been an integral part of life. The Bible tells us in the book of Genesis that when God created the earth, it was full of only good things—stars and seas, fish and fowl, vegetation and vertebrates.

As God's crowning act of creation, he molded some earth as a potter shapes clay, then breathed life into it. This first human, Adam (Hebrew for "man"), reflected God's image, as have all persons since. The first man and his wife, Eve, were given dominion over the earth and its creatures.

God also gave Adam and Eve free reign over the lush garden of Eden, with one exception: "You must not eat from the tree of the knowledge of good and evil, for when you eat of it you will surely die."

Then Satan, a fallen angel disguised as a serpent, slithered up to the woman, and incited rebellion. The snake asked, "Did God really say, 'You must not eat from any tree in the garden'?"

Eve pondered the question. She knew the fruit looked appealing; and she thought it could make her morally independent of God. So she tasted it, then offered some to her husband. Adam promptly chomped on the ripe fruit as well, ignoring the foreboding consequences.

Those consequences were swift and far-reaching. With those bites, the couple broke harmony with their creator. Suddenly they realized their nakedness and felt ashamed. They hastily plucked leaves from a nearby fig tree and pieced together coverings.

Entrance of Shame

In the evening, Adam and Eve heard God walking in the garden, and they felt doubly ashamed. This time they dodged behind some trees.

"Where are you?" called God, the way a mother calls a toddler who has clapped hands over his eyes and "hidden."

Adam replied, "I heard you in the garden, and I was afraid because I was naked; so I hid."

"Who told you that you were naked?" asked God. "Have you eaten from the tree that I commanded you not to eat from?"

Adam shrugged, saying, "The woman you put here with me—she gave me some fruit from the tree, and I ate." Eve, in turn, blamed the snake. God punished all three.

First, God cursed Satan, saying he would eventually be overcome by the woman's offspring (Jesus). Next, God said Eve would experience pain in childbirth. Then he said Adam would till the soil in pain, and he and Eve would eventually die, returning to the dust. All of these prophecies came true.

Adam and Eve's sin—often called the "original sin"—is the source of all pain in this world. The Bible says, "Sin entered the world through one man, and death through sin, and in this way death came to all men, because all sinned" (Romans 5:12).

Yet in his judgment, God also showed mercy. He did not kill Adam and Eve, but clothed them with animal skins before banishing them from the garden. In this way, he covered their sin. Later, God sent his only Son, Jesus Christ, into the world to wipe away the sins of humanity. Read more about this in "The Choice Is Yours," on pages 71–72.

The account of Adam and Eve, found in Genesis 1–3, isn't just about the origin of sin and pain. It is the first of many descriptions of how God lovingly seeks a relationship with humanity—and how we've constantly rebelled.

Your Thoughts

1. Take a few moments to reflect on how evil entered the world.

   a. On a scale of "1," indicating "don't believe," to "5," indicating "completely believe," designate the extent to which you believe this story from the Bible.

   1   2   3   4   5

   b. Why did you respond this way?

2. The Bible claims to be God's words to humanity. Read the following verse. What would help you believe this claim and follow the Bible's truths?

   All Scripture is God-breathed and is useful for teaching, rebuking, correcting and training. (2 Timothy 3:16)

3. Think about your life: thoughts, words, actions. Is there evidence that you've disobeyed God and tried to cover your sin? Explain.

4. What would cause you to take seriously your sin before God?

Spiritual Vacuum

Some people describe the effect of original sin as a "spiritual vacuum." In the February 1991 issue of *Life* magazine, Lee Atwater, former chairman of the Republican National Committee, talked about his battle with an inoperable brain tumor.

The "before" and "after" photographs of this once ruthless and cocky political strategist show how quickly circumstances can change us. Atwater's fight with cancer brought a new reliance on God, a peace in a tumultuous situation. Here is an excerpt from his story:

> *Long before I was struck with cancer, I felt something stirring in American society. It was a sense among the people of the country – Republicans and Democrats alike – that something was missing from their lives, something crucial.*
>
> *I was trying to position the Republican Party to take advantage of it. But I wasn't exactly sure what "it" was. My illness helped me see that what was missing in society was missing in me: a little heart, a lot of brotherhood.*
>
> *The '80s were about acquiring – acquiring wealth, power, prestige. I know. I acquired more wealth, power and prestige than most. But you can acquire all you want and still feel empty.*
>
> *It took a deadly illness to put me eye to eye with that truth, but it is a truth that the country, caught up in its ruthless ambitions and moral decay, can learn on my dime. I don't know who will lead us through the '90s, but*

*they must be made to speak to this spiritual
vacuum at the heart of American society, this
tumor of the soul.*[1]

God to the Rescue

5. Read the following Bible chapter:

*Out of the depths I cry to you, O LORD; O Lord,
hear my voice. Let your ears be attentive to my
cry for mercy.*

*If you, O LORD, kept a record of sins, O
Lord, who could stand? But with you there is
forgiveness; therefore you are feared.*

*I wait for the LORD, my soul waits, and in
his word I put my hope. My soul waits for the
Lord more than watchmen wait for the morning,
more than watchmen wait for the morning.*

*O Israel, put your hope in the LORD, for
with the LORD is unfailing love and with him
is full redemption. He himself will redeem Israel
from all their sins.* (Psalm 130)

a. What does the psalmist who wrote this
   acknowledge about himself?

b. Where does he find hope?

c. How does he describe God?

d. What does God want to do for his people?

6. How would you like God to respond to your sin? ■

NOTE
  1. Lee Atwater with Todd Brewster, "Lee Atwater's Last Campaign," *Life* magazine, February 1991, pages 86-87.

The Choice Is Yours

You can receive the ultimate comfort.

I n this booklet, you've explored various aspects of pain. And in "More Than a Myth" on pages 63-69, you studied the spiritual vacuum caused by sin that separates us from God. Just as no one is immune from pain, so no one is immune from sin. Or, as Romans 3:23 puts it, "All have sinned and fall short of the glory of God."

Although God was saddened by Adam and Eve's sin and punished their actions, he provided animal skins to cover their nakedness. Similarly, Jesus Christ was God's ultimate provision to cover our nakedness.

The Bible calls Jesus "the lamb of God," because at that time in history, lambs were sacrificed for people's sins. Because he was perfect, Jesus' death paid the price for all sin: Adam's, Eve's, yours, mine. Not only did he pay for our sins, but he restored our relationship with God.

A Woman's Right

Today, people talk about "a woman's right to choose." In regard to a relationship with God, he has always allowed us the privilege of choice (theologians call this "free will"). God wants us to accept him freely, not out of force. Sometimes our choices hurt him and us, but he allows us the right, nonetheless.

Isaiah 45:22 says, "Turn to me and be saved." God's salvation is that simple. *Salvation* means that God fills our vacuum with his Spirit and cancels spiritual death by granting us eternal life in heaven.

As we saw in lesson 1, while Jesus was dying on the cross, one criminal being crucified beside him turned his eyes toward God's only Son. After admitting he deserved to die, the criminal said, "Jesus, remember me when you come into your kingdom."

Jesus looked at the criminal with compassion and said, "I tell you the truth, today you will be with me in paradise" (Luke 23:42-43).

In the same way, if you look to God and repent for the sin that has separated you from him, he will forgive you and fill you with new life through his Spirit. You need no magic formula, only a humble heart.

Having read this booklet, you know that I didn't escape pain just because I asked God into my life. But I hope you also know that God has poured out his love and helped me through the pain. I pray that you, too, will know God's comfort and new life.

The choice is yours. ■

Hope and Help for Sufferers

Resources for those in pain.

Carter, Les. *The Prodigal Spouse.* Nashville, TN: Thomas Nelson, 1990.

Cermak, Dr. Timmen L. *Time to Heal: The Road to Recovery for Adult Children of Alcoholics.* New York: Avon Books, 1988.

Elliot, Elisabeth. *A Path Through Suffering.* Ann Arbor, MI: Servant Publications, 1990.

Elliot, Elisabeth. *Loneliness.* Nashville, TN: Oliver-Nelson Books, 1988.

Hemfelt, Dr. Robert, Dr. Frank Minirth, and Dr. Paul Meier. *Love Is a Choice: Recovery for Codependent Relationships.* Nashville, TN: Thomas Nelson, 1989.

Lee, Laurel. *Walking Through the Fire.* New York: Bantam Books, 1978.

Lewis, C. S. *A Grief Observed.* New York: Bantam Books, 1961.

Lewis, C. S. *The Problem of Pain*. New York: Macmillan, 1962.

Minirth, Dr. Frank, Dr. Paul Meier, Dr. Robert Hemfelt, and Dr. Sharon Sneed. *Love Hunger: Recovery for Food Codependency*. Nashville, TN: Thomas Nelson, 1990.

Veninga, Robert. *A Gift of Hope: How We Survive Our Tragedies*. Boston, MA: Little, Brown & Co., 1983.

Walters, Candace. *Invisible Wounds: What Every Woman Should Know About Sexual Assault*. Portland, OR: Multnomah Press, 1987.

Yancey, Philip. *Disappointment with God: Three Questions No One Asks Aloud*. Grand Rapids, MI: Zondervan, 1988.

Yancey, Philip. *Where Is God When It Hurts?* Grand Rapids, MI: Zondervan, 1977. ∎

A lice Lawson Cox has always said she could "write *the book* on pain," but this is her first attempt. When not contemplating such serious subjects, she likes to blow bubbles, walk on the beach, and explore monuments in nearby Washington, D.C.

A former senior writer for Prison Fellowship Ministries, Lawson has published several freelance articles. Two of her feature stories have won awards from the Evangelical Press Association.

Lawson is currently pursuing a master's degree in education, with hopes of teaching elementary-aged children. In her free moments, she is discovering God in fresh ways with the help of her third-grade Sunday school class. ■

ther study booklets in the *QUESTIONS WOMEN ASK* series are:

Can I Really Have It All? by Maxine Hancock. Discover the real meaning of success and fulfillment.

If I'm So Good, Why Don't I Act That Way? by Judith Couchman. Face the frustration of not being who you'd like to be.

If My Kids Drive Me Crazy, Am I a Bad Mom? by Janet Chester Bly. How to make the most of the mothering years.

Is Your To-Do List About to Do You In? by Marlene LeFever. Sort out and reduce the stresses of everyday living.

Why Do I Always Play It So Safe? by Evelyn Bence. Move past your fears toward the freedom to pursue your dreams.

These studies can be purchased at a Christian bookstore. Or order a catalog from NavPress, Customer Services, P. O. Box 6000, Colorado Springs, CO 80934. Or call 1-800-366-7788 for information. ■